BEADLE'S DIME BOOK
OF PRACTICAL ETIQUETTE
FOR LADIES AND GENTLEMEN

BEADLE'S DIME BOOK
OF PRACTICAL ETIQUETTE
FOR LADIES AND GENTLEMEN

BEING A GUIDE TO TRUE GENTILITY AND GOOD-BREEDING, AND A COMPLETE DIRECTORY TO THE USAGES AND OBSERVANCES OF SOCIETY.

BY

ANONYMOUS

INCLUDING

Etiquette of the Ball Room, of the Evening Party, the Dinner-Party, the Card and Chess Table, of Business, of the Home Circle, &c., &c.

PREPARED EXPRESSLY FOR THE "DIME SERIES"
BY A COMMITTEE OF THREE.

CONTENTS

LOVE, COURTSHIP, AND MARRIAGE.

RESPECT FOR RELIGION AND FOR OLD AGE.

SPECIAL WORD, FOR LADIES ONLY.

CONFIDENTIAL ADVICE TO YOUNG MEN.

CULTIVATE A TASTE FOR THE BEAUTIFUL.

ETIQUETTE OF HORSEBACK RIDING.

THE LAWS OF HOME ETIQUETTE.

CARDS OF INVITATION, WEDDING CARDS, ETC.

INTRODUCTION.

"THAT man is a gentleman!" How the heart opens to let him in, without any further commendation! He may be wise, and rich, and remarked for his genius; but if he be not a true gentleman, his gifts will not avail to make him a favorite and a desirable companion.

"That woman is a lady!" What matter, then, if she is not clad in silks, or is not beautiful of form or feature? She has the key which unlocks all hearts for her, for to be a lady, implies high qualities and gracious gifts of soul.

Why, then, are not all persons gentlemen and ladies? We can not tell, except it be that some, and a large class of, persons look upon politeness as something effeminate, or as fit only for fops; and therefore make boors of themselves, because it is so manly to be coarse and to do just as one pleases. Some are actually ignorant of what constitutes true politeness, and err not from willfulness, but from want of knowledge. But such persons are readily forgivable, for, if their disposition is to be polite, they will find the way very easy into the confidence of all, and will learn, ere long, what custom and usage has sanctioned as fit and proper regulations for the intercourse of men with men, women with women, and all with one another.

It is to such persons as those last-named, that we especially address this little manual. To learn the usages of society is easy, if one only *will* learn; for, after all, these usages are not complicated and burdensome, but grounded upon simplicity itself: the great law which underlies all, is the blessed Golden Rule:

"Do unto others as ye would that they should do unto you."

We propose to give such suggestions, in the various departments of social experience, as will advise the reader of the usages sanctioned by eminent authority, and of the deportment proper and acceptable to well-bred persons; and flatter ourselves that, if our advice is followed, this "DIME BOOK OF ETIQUETTE" will prove entirely competent to fit its attentive reader to move with credit and self-respect in any circle where a true lady or gentleman always finds ready recognition.

BEADLE'S DIME BOOK OF ETIQUETTE.

ENTRANCE INTO SOCIETY.

General Observations—Case of the Bashful Young Man—Enter Society Early—Avoid Forwardness and Romping—Snobs—Fops—Bores—The Secret of Making Yourself at Ease—Good-Nature everything,

HAS the moment arrived when you are called upon to cast aside your youthful associations and youthful irresponsibilities to take your place in society as a man or woman? It is a most important moment—one which deserves the consideration of a thoughtful study; for, upon a proper knowledge of what belongs to true manhood, true womanhood, does much of your after-life success depend. If you are ignorant of the laws of politeness, of the rules and observances of true sociality, of the means necessary to render yourself an agreeable companion and a useful member of the social circle, you begin life at immense disadvantage, and will never cease to regret that ignorance. It is such an easy matter to become familiar with the usages and proprieties of social life that ignorance is inexcusable; and when we see men of sense and sagacity behaving, in an assembly, at a party, at the dinner-table, at the card-table, like half-tutored savages,—rude, awkward, uncivil, a source of annoyance to their friends, we feel a degree of indignation rather than of pity, since it is so easy to learn how to behave, that there really is no good excuse for boorishness and awkward deportment.

To illustrate, let us narrate the case of our young friend Falconbridge, whose *entree* into society afforded a subject of laughter and comment for weeks after the incidents which he has had the courage to place before us as a warning. He tells his story thus:

"I pulled the bell with a most nervous twitch; I 'walked in' with fear and misgivings; in the parlor not only sat Miss Jones, but her two cousins, the old lady, a maiden aunt, and some four or five of the junior branches of the Jones family. I got through, though it was fearful work. I set my hat on the center-table, and it fell off; I picked it up, and in doing so, hit my nose against a pile of gilt-edged literature, and down it came pell-mell; but the children came to my rescue, and I finally found myself armed by a lady each side—the cousins! Imagine my feelings—Miss J. going in advance, *en route,* down the avenue to the portly residence of Misses

Degrands. We entered the vestibule; I had not spoken a word all the way; the two pretty cousins and Miss J. doing a heap of conversation. In the hall the old negro servant made a grab at my hat, but I held on, and in triumph carried it into the parlor, where, in the midst of introductions, flaring of lamps, and waving and fluttering of silks and cashmeres, bowing, scraping, fuss and feathers, to all of which I was more or less deaf and blind, down upon a piano-stool in the corner I dropped my hat.

"The two cousins froze to me, introduced me; I bowed; one of the Miss Degrands came forward; I was introduced, and as she, in the tip of fashion, made her perfectly grand theatrical bow to me, grabbed her by the hand in the most democratic manner imaginable, and shook it most heartily. She not only blushed, but, by her eyes, I saw that she was likewise mad as a hornet. Her sister and her had a word, and then her sister avoided me. Things grew no better fast; from one bungle I got into another. In *whist* I was ignorant and awkward; in a hop waltz with one of the cousins, I trod on her toes, until she screamed; and, in trying to mend the matter, I stepped on the flounces of Miss Degrand's dress and tore off five yards at least. In despair, I backed down, saw a seat, rushed to it, and down I sat upon my hat! In confusion I arose, snatched up the pancake-looking affair, which I frenziedly held up to public gaze. There was a roar of laughter—in which I did not join, I assure you; I gave a rush forward, hit the corner of the table, tilted over the astral lamp!—such a crash!—I kept on, I made for the door which just then old Degrand was entering *avant courier* of his old negro man, who bore a large tray well filled with wine in glasses. I struck the old gentleman so forcibly that he fell upon Pompey, glasses, and wine; and, on my mad career, I proceeded. Going out the wrong end of the hall, I found myself in a dark dining-room; but, jerking open the first door in advance, I went out into a hall, thence to an anteroom; groping in the dark, I struck my forehead against a half-open door, saw bushels of stars, and—*fell senseless!*

"How or when I got home, the Lord only knows; but, for one week, I had a head too big for my hat, and a pair of terrifically black eyes. As soon as able to travel, I left that 'settlement' never to return."

Now this is no overwrought scene, but one which could easily have happened to any bashful, awkward, disconcerted young person. The great error he made was in not going into society perfectly *self-possessed*, from having a right knowledge of what was proper in company. In the first place, he had *waited too long* before entering into society, and, secondly, he had not informed himself at all upon the most common proprieties of the parlor. What else could have been expected than discomfiture and disgrace?

As a rule, then, let us recommend all young persons to enter into social intercourse ere they become "of age." It is a most admirable experience to meet in friendly chat with a friend or two—to spend an evening with an intelligent lady, and to learn by degrees the confidence and reliance which will serve to carry you bravely through the evening at the brilliant rooms of fashion and gay company. It will be found, by both sexes, that timidity wears off rapidly by simple social converse; and the young man or woman who proposes to become a gentleman or lady should not fail to embrace every opportunity for meeting with well-mannered and intelligent friends—to spend an evening with them—to read, talk, walk, ride with them—to go out to concerts, to the theater, to the pic-nic, excursion, church, or evening party.

Timidity is not a sin—it is merely a *fault* which will soon wear away, and a proper self-possession will take its place, if the novice in society will use all necessary means to overcome the feeling which takes fright at a smile, and is disconcerted by a frown.

In seeking to overcome bashfulness, let there be a careful study to avoid the very common extreme of forwardness. This is the more unbearable because it is a sin of commission, while bashfulness is a sin of omission. To be forward, rude, intrusive, argues a sad want of good breeding which no leniency will overlook. In a female this rudeness is absolutely unbearable, because it so outrages all ideas of feminine graces and virtues—it makes us think the person *coarse*, and this very feeling divests us of the respect, the reverence which should always be felt for the "gentle sex." We say earnestly to those young girls who bandy words with provoking young men, who always romp when they are abroad, and win the name of being "independent," that you very much injure yourself in the estimation of all well-mannered persons, and do your character the injustice of having it considered *un*-feminine. Be gay, be cheerful, be the spirit of every company, but at the same time preserve the delicacy, the refinement, the grace, which are the surest virtues for conquering admiration, for winning love.

"Snobs" are always impudent, and generally are ignorant persons. They are rude as the monkey is rude, because they really do not know what constitutes good breeding. Their tailor literally "makes the man"—their whole mind is given to the tie of their cravat, and their boots absorb much of their hardest efforts at philosophy. They are simply nuisances—a blot on the fair name of man, and should be regarded as an *extensive* species of ape.

"Fops" are not always "snobs." A person may be very vain of dress, and make a silly display of dry goods and jewelry, and still be very genteel and perfectly polished in manners. The love of show is a strong passion in a larger class of persons than is generally supposed, for many who do not wear the latest styles still have peculiarities of dress or ornament which are the result of as great a degree of vanity as besets the more gaudily dressed. It is a weakness to be vain of dress, for it places a virtue in goods which does not belong to it—it elevates a perishable and purchasable commodity above the truer and nobler attributes of mind.

"Bores" are a large class, and number such a variety of species as to baffle definition. Let it suffice for us to say, a man or woman is a bore when they are *intruders*, either upon persons' time or company. To know when to leave, when to cease conversation, when to offer attentions, to solicit favors, is to know how to behave well; and no person will err who is educated in gentility, or whose apprehension of what is right is not befogged by "charming illusions." One of the worst bores we ever met was a female, who acted as a kind of purveyor-general to the community for every charity which called for an active benevolence. This lady would come into our study at any moment, would force us into hearing which we did not wish to hear, and into giving what we did not conscientiously think it right to give—so great was her faculty for "talking things into a person." She and her friends thought her a very valuable woman; we then thought her to be, and now know her to have been, a most unmitigated bore of the "benevolent" school.

We have here described these several enemies of good breeding, because we do not wish to recur to them again: let us here beg of our readers to make such application of the suggestions as will prevent any of them from becoming either "snobs," "fops," or "bores."

Once in the presence of company, large or small, forget yourself so far as to become *one of the number*—lose yourself, your hands, and feet, and eyes, in the feeling of non-individualism, without which there really can be no real enjoyment. What is called *abandon* is a sense of non-individuality—a forgetfulness of self so far as to enter keenly into the spirit of the time and occasion. Give yourself no particular *anxiety* about your person, your demeanor, your words and ways: you can, if not perfectly "at home," have a care to demean yourself well and creditably; but do not be anxious about it, for anxiety breeds a disquiet which is fatal to enjoyment and to a good impression upon others. Good-nature is every thing in society, as in business—it overcomes many a mountain of difficulty, and achieves a success where no sternness or anxious solicitude would avail.

In regard to the formulas of introductions, cards of invitation, etc., too much stress is laid by writers upon etiquette, who leave the impression that there is a whole chapter of Greek verbs to learn before the debutant in society can become familiar with necessary forms. There is little, indeed, to cause alarm, the forms being just what any person's common-sense would dictate as being proper. We will give, in the chapter succeeding, such general observances and formulas for introductions, etc., as seem necessary to "post" our readers upon the subject.

GENERAL OBSERVANCES, INTRODUCTIONS, ETC.

The several Kinds of Visits—Styles of Dress appropriate—Proper Time to Call—Make a brief Stay—Visits to the Newly-Married—Of Condolence—After a Party—on New Year's day, etc.,

Among the gentilities of life, visits hold a first place, and deserve attention. Their various occasion, their different character and purpose, their meaning are multiple, and have, therefore, some forms necessary to be preserved. We may remark that visits are classified as follows, viz.: visits of mere form and policy; visits of real friendship; visits of congratulation and of condolence; visits to give out invitations for dinner, or a dance, or an evening party; visits of state, where the party called upon is a "lion," an eminent person, etc., etc.

The general style of dress to be adopted upon all these occasions, is one of studied neatness rather than of display or of elegance. Display upon such occasions is really vulgar—it should be reserved for the gay and brilliant soiree or evening company, if it is made at all.

The *time* for the visit is *after* twelve o'clock, noon; before that hour the lady of the house is supposed to be busy at her household duties, and in getting the rooms in order for the day: never make a call before that hour.

Occupy but a brief time in your call, for you know not how much the lady of the house may have to do, nor where she may wish to go, hence it is best always to make your call brief. If strongly urged to remain longer, it would be impolite to go in haste; but, as a general thing, let fifteen or twenty minutes be the time spent in the visit. You will not then be voted a "bore," but, on the other hand, will be considered a pleasant caller—particularly if you have made yourself agreeable.

Should another person be announced or enter on a visit before your own visit is finished, it is but proper for you immediately to retire, unless you may be intimate with both the host and the new-comer, and are invited to remain. Otherwise be not precipitate to leave, but politely withdraw, for you do not know what "confidences" there may be to be talked over.

Visits of congratulation upon occasion of marriage, or safe return from a journey, or long absence, or escape from calamity, should be at as early a moment as the party seems ready for such visits; and should be always made when you entertain a regard for the person interested. It is now the practice for newly-married people to send out their cards to those of their old friends with whom they wish to renew acquaintance in their new relationships; and it is a sign that you do not wish to renew the acquaintance if you fail to respond to the card by calling. If you fail to call, the parties can not consistently recognize you afterward, except you have some good and sufficient apology to offer for your absence from their reception-rooms.

Visits of condolence are too much neglected in this "fast" country of ours. In Europe the custom of calling upon those who have suffered a loss by death is quite general. The call, of course, should be brief, and the words offered of the kindest and most considerate character. It will greatly relieve the pangs of sorrow for the living to feel that others are solicitous for their welfare.

After you have attended a party, soiree, or sociable, it is proper to call upon your host within a fortnight, to make inquiries after his or her health, and to re-mark upon the pleasure you experienced on the occasion of the party. This is a pleasant way of showing your friends that their efforts to please you are appreci-ated.

New Year visits, strangely enough, are not general in this country outside of a few large cities. The first day of the New Year is set apart for general "calls," when houses are "open," and all are privileged to enter who are friends of the host, or who are in company with a person who is on the calling list of the house. It is *not* proper for a perfect stranger to enter a room and introduce himself to the ladies present, just because the door is "open;" if you wish to call upon the receivers of company, get some proper friend to introduce you. Even the freedom of New Year's day will not excuse a liberty with strangers.

In many instances houses are not open to "calls," on New Year's day, for var-ious reasons. In cases of this kind, it is a pleasant reminder of your existence, and of your wish to continue your social relations for the year, to send in your card sometime during January, or, what is better, to call sometime during the month, and re-establish yourself in the list of friends of the party.

SPECIAL OBSERVANCES FOR ALL OCCA-SIONS

Directions for all to Learn by Heart, in Regard to Dress, Demeanor, Conversation, etc., etc.,

Of the various *technicalities* of these several occasions, we may say:

Never forget to enter the room with thoroughly-cleaned boots. Always use the scraper and mats at the door.

If you meet any one on the staircase, you should uncover, whoever it may be. You should do the same in case of an introduction.

If you have a cane, keep it in your hand, and be careful not to make much noise with your boots.

When a new visitor enters a drawing-room, if it be a gentleman, the ladies bow slightly; if a lady, every one rises.

Beware of asking the hour, or of taking out your watch during a visit; avoid spitting on the floor—your pocket-handkerchief will serve your purpose. To place your hat on any article of furniture when you enter a room is ungenteel; to lay it on a bed is unpardonable. You must hold it in your hand, or leave it with your over-coat in the anteroom. Crossing the legs, and stretching them out at full length, are equally improper.

The last arrival in a drawing-room takes a seat left vacant near the mistress of the house.

A lady is not required to rise on receiving a gentleman, nor to accompany him to the door.

If you are invited to lay down your hat, place it beside, *not* before you.

A *young* man will avoid sitting in an arm-chair—which should always be awarded to the ladies or old gentlemen present. Leave the seat next the fire to superiors in age or position. The children of the family should assist their parents in receiving visitors, relieve the ladies of their wrappings, provide seats, and ac-company to the door.

Never look about you in a room, as if you were making an inventory.

The gloves should not be removed during a visit. To brush your hat with your hand will expose you to the charge of extreme vulgarity.

At the entrance of a visitor you should rise. A professional man in his office is alone exempted from this custom.

A lady does not put her address on her visiting-card. We may here also add these further general hints and suggestions:

Naturalness is an essential item in good-breeding. Hear what La Bruyere thinks on this important question: "Some young people do not sufficiently understand the advantages of natural charms, and how much they would gain by trusting to them entirely. They weaken these gifts of heaven, so rare and fragile, by affected manners and an awkward imitation. Their tones and their gait are borrowed; they study their attitudes before the glass, until they have lost all trace of natural manner, and, with all their pains, they please but little."

Without being vain, a young girl should be careful of her person. Nothing is more repugnant to good taste, than an air of neglect in the toilet and deportment of woman. The hair and head-dress especially require care and neatness.

Beware of imitating those people who never know what to do with their bodies, and can never keep their hands quiet.

Swinging on one's chair is extremely ill-bred.

The eye-glass stuck in the eye, denotes either the dandy, the clerk, or the student. This custom is in no way disagreeable to the passers-by, but it has an air of ill-breeding and impertinence.

To follow a lady in the street, and turn the head to stare at her, is still more impertinent than to do so in a promenade, especially in cities, for reasons which can not be further averted to in a book intended for young persons of both sexes.

Familiarity with servants should be avoided, but they should always be addressed with civility.

Some people, in speaking to you, have a silly habit of passing their hand through the hair, or stroking the mustache; some even carry a pocket-comb, which they produce on all occasions, for dressing the beard; others bite their nails, play with their watch-key, or jingle the money in their pocket; all these offences against propriety denote a want of good-breeding.

Excess in perfume should be avoided, lest the suspicion be excited that you deal in the odors that you inhale.

Good-sense has often more to do than education, in making a polished man.

One of the essential qualities of good-breeding, is deserving general esteem by one's deportment.

In little social games, a malicious girl will sometimes amuse herself by imposing on a companion a forfeit that will make her ridiculous; this shows a bad disposition of mind as well as ill-breeding.

If, in offering a lady a gift, you select one that is very costly, you may be guilty of an impertinence.

To speak in society of private matters, is extremely improper.

Turning up the sleeves on sitting down to table, as some persons do, is gross in the highest degree.

A habit of swearing always marks a vulgar man.

Calling to the waiter with a loud voice in a public-room, and striking violently on the table, are indicative of extreme ignorance.

A snuff-taker should not take out his box at table; his neighbor will be little pleased at receiving the stray grains in his plate.

Indiscreet questions are impertinent, as well as unseasonable harangues.

You should be ready to act the knight, if a lady in your company is attacked. If she give offence, and that without reason, your office is that of mediator. You should even ask pardon for your companion. A bully would act otherwise; but it is absurd to get into a quarrel for the sake of maintaining that a person who is in-solent has a right to be so, and that because he is of your company. You will show yourself, in acting thus, as ill-bred as he.

If, in doing an obliging act, you make people feel the obligation, you deprive it entirely of its value.

If you speak of a friend to a person who is not intimate with both him and you, preface his name with the word Mr. It would not be proper to say to a servant or a porter, "Is Julius here?" You must say, "Is Mr. Julius here?"

A servant who understands propriety, always speaks of his superiors in the third person.

When you receive a present, it would be an offence to the donor to dismiss the porter without a gratuity.

If the honor of a woman be attacked, you should always defend it. It is not allowable for any one to assail the reputation of a lady, even if she be open to censure.

In walking with a lady in the street, leave her the inner side of the pavement. If you meet friends in a narrow passage, or on a footpath, be careful not to block up the way. It would be very impolite to inconvenience the passers-by in this manner.

In whatever society you are, it is unpardonable to remain covered in the pres-ence of a lady. Louis XIV., going one day on foot out of the castle of Versailles, uncovered before a vender of cakes who was stationed near the gate. The courtiers having expressed their surprise; "Gentlemen," said the monarch, "is not the king's mother a woman?" Our readers may also remember the incident related of Henry Clay: a negro woman courtesied to him, when he raised his hat politely to her in return. "What!" said a friend, "do you recognize negroes?" The noble reply was: "I never allow negroes to excel me in good manners."

When your visitor retires, you should accompany him to the anteroom, and save him the trouble of opening the door. In the case of a lady or an old gentleman, it is proper to go to the foot of the staircase.

THE FORMULA OF INTRODUCTIONS.

How to "Introduce" — General Forms to be Observed — When Introductions are Proper — Promiscuous Introductions Improper,

We shall say only a few words about presentations. The same form is always observed, "Let me introduce to you Mr. B.;" or, "Mr. Jones, allow me to present to you Mr. Smith;" or, "I have the honor to present to you my intimate friend." Introduce no person until you are sure it is agreeable to *both* parties. Ladies should always be asked if they wish to know Mr. — — ere he is presented to them. The rule *invariably* is, to introduce gentlemen *to* ladies — *not* ladies *to* gentlemen. Or, in case of men to men, always present the younger *to* the older — the lesser *to* the greater. We Americans, in our disregard of rank and position, are too apt to overlook the courtesies established among gentlemen. The person thus presented bows, the host repeats the oft-spoken compliment, and, with a graceful rejoinder, the ceremony concludes.

Both ladies and gentlemen should be careful about introducing persons to each other, without being first satisfied that such a course will be mutually agreeable.

The custom in this country, particularly among gentlemen, of indiscriminate introductions, is carried to such a ridiculous extent, that it has often been made the subject of comment by foreigners, who can discover no possible advantage in being made acquainted with others with whom they are not likely to associate for three minutes, in whom they take not the slightest interest, and whom they probably will never again encounter, nor recognize if they should. Besides, every one has a right to exercise his own judgment and taste in the selection of acquaintances, and it is clearly a breach of politeness to thrust them upon your friend or associate, without knowing whether it Will be agreeable to either party.

ON DRESS AND ORNAMENTS.

Good Dress highly Proper and Necessary—The kind of Garments proper for Various Occasions—Jewelry and "Flash" Dressing vulgar—When Jewelry is in Good Taste—Special advice to Females upon Their Dress—Flowers, Jewels, Feathers, Arrangement of Hair, etc., etc.,

A man is judged of by his appearance, and seldom incorrectly. A neat exterior, equally free from extravagance and poverty, always proclaims a right-minded and sensible man. To dress appropriately, and with good taste, is to respect yourself and others.

A black coat and trowsers are indispensable for a visit of ceremony, an entertainment, an evening party, or a ball. The white or black vest is equally proper in any of these cases. *Very ceremonious* visits require a dress shoe and a white vest. The hand should always be gloved on such occasions. Always wear kids in dancing. A gentleman, when in dress and out of his business, should also walk out gloved. One hand may be uncovered; the one you will extend if you meet an acquaintance.

If it be not well-bred for a gentleman out of business hours to appear in the street or at church without gloves, it is still less so for a lady.

Rings and heavy gold chains are *not* in good taste. Some young persons, of both sexes, have a strong desire to sport gold and jewels; but let them remember that such is the taste of gamblers and courtesans, and they may realize how really vulgar is too much jewelry.

To a woman, the toilet is indeed a study, to which she should devote a proper portion of her time; and, sure of being well-skilled in the art, she is impatient of the observations of the critic. All do not, however, escape the charge of vulgarity. We sometimes see dresses in which the ill-assorted or showy colors spoil the effect of the richest material. The various articles of dress must be well-chosen, so as to produce an agreeable *harmony*. Never put on a dark-colored bonnet with a light, spring costume. Avoid uniting colors which will suggest an epigram—such as a straw-colored dress, with a green bonnet. [Of the last-named style of headgear you must especially beware, unless you have an extremely fair complexion; otherwise your malicious rivals will assert that your face resembles a citron, surrounded by its foliage.] The arrangements of the hair is an important affair. Bands are becoming to faces of a Grecian cast—while ringlets better suit those lively and expressive heads which resemble the beautiful Ninon. But, whatever be your style of countenance, avoid a cumbrous edifice of lace mixed with hair, and let your flowers be few and choice. A spray or two of heath, the delicate blossoms of the jessamine, violets—orange blossoms, a white rose—these simple ornaments are most suitable to a young girl, and even of these she should not be too prodigal, for beauty *unadorned* is adorned the most.

In a married woman, a richer style of ornament is admissible. Feathers in her bonnet, a necklace, a camellia or jewels in her hair are allowable in the wife, but for a young girl, a style of modest simplicity is far more impressive and becoming. We shall state what is known to be a fact, when we say ladies who attract most observation, are those dressed with the most studied simplicity, while those with most ornament are treated with less deference, and excite less compliment.

An important maxim to be observed is, that the most elegant dress loses its merit, if it is not worn with grace. Young girls often have an air of constraint, and their dress seems to partake of their want of ease. The celebrated Sappho is said to have attended to the arrangement even of the folds of her mantle. She is indeed fortunate, who can give an easy flexibility to her figure, and graceful movements to her head: she will always appear graceful and well-dressed.

There are women whose dress is extravagant—folly of this kind should be avoided: a simple style of dress is ever *proof* of modesty, and one never loses by appearing to be modest.

For many valuable recipes for the toilet, and hints and suggestions in reference to the complexion, the hair, the teeth, etc., see "BEADLE'S DIME RECIPE BOOK."

ON CLEANLINESS AND FASTIDIOUSNESS.

**The Hands, Nails, Mouth, Teeth, etc., etc.—Bathe Frequently for
Purity of Complexion—Tobacco and Smell of Smoke Offensive
and Forbidden in the House or in the Presence of Ladies—"Broken" garments—Neatness inseparable from True Gentility,**

If there be one thing that we should recommend more than another, it is cleanliness. We might, indeed, abstain from this caution, upon the supposition that the
reader can not stand in need of it. But, to clear our conscience, we devote a chapter
to the subject. The hands should receive special attention, as they serve for a spec-
imen of the rest. Every morning wash them with plenty of soap and water, then
with the brush, clean your nails, cut them, and beware of the dark crescent which
gets the name of half-mourning; nothing can be more disgusting. Let your face
and neck be clean; we particularly recommend attention to the ears.

Rinse your mouth often; in the morning, to remove the impurities of the night;
after dinner, to avoid making others acquainted with the meats you have partaken
of; and at night, before retiring to rest, that you may sleep more sweetly. If you are
given to the really filthy habit of using tobacco, in *any* shape, *never* appear in any
social circle, or to any friend for whom you have any respect, with the *odor* of the
stuff about you. Let your use of it be as much in secret as possible. No gentleman
will ever smoke a cigar where its smoke can give the least offence. In Boston smoking is positively prohibited in the streets: it should be in every city.

Frequent baths are absolutely necessary, and still more, frequent foot-baths,
with tepid water and soap; for the dust that one acquires in walking, changes its
name at the end of three days, and in making a call, your friends will be aware of
your presence before they have seen you. Let your hat and clothes be carefully
brushed.

Nothing is more disagreeable in either sex, than soiled shoes or stockings. It
shows either great negligence or uncleanliness. Let your linen be perfectly white,
and your dress spotless.

How often do we see women walking in the street with a torn or frayed dress,
or a *broken* stocking. Idleness alone is the cause of such things; it is *so* easy to stop
a rent, and certainly it can not be said that thread is dear.

A dress ever so simple, and cheap, if it be neat, is preferable to finery and dirt:
one is respectable, the other is not.

In the pocket-handkerchief great nicety should be observed, both from regard
to appearances, and for the sake of personal comfort. It should be white and al-

ways clean. A dirty handkerchief is an abomination. A drop of perfume on it will make it all the pleasanter to yourself and to others.

Perfect cleanliness in *all* things gives one a feeling of self-respect. It not only affords an agreeable sensation of comfort, but imparts an air of confidence, springing from the consciousness that you need not fear the investigations or ridicule of any who approach you. It will procure you an acquittal for many little defects of heart, or mind, or temper, and win you respect where you may least expect to make a favorable impression.

CONVERSATION AND PERSONAL ADDRESS.

The Various Talkers—How to Talk and When—The kind of Subjects proper to Introduce—Pedantry out of Place—Impropriety of Personalities—Good Talking and Good Manners always go Together

It is rare to meet with persons who can converse agreeably; and yet how many kinds of talkers there are in the world. First comes the man who details his own adventures, bringing in even his boyish escapades, in order to keep up the continuous discharge; the gastronomic talker, who regales you with a description of famous dishes; the detailer of empty trifles; the exquisite Leander of every hysterical dame; the universal grumbler, who sees nothing of the sun but its spots; the self-constituted reporter of every kind of scandal; with many others too numerous to mention.

If you wish to make yourself agreeable to a lady, turn the conversation adroitly upon taste, or art, or books, or persons, or events of the day. Make her smile—suffer her to be superior in any encounter of wit—and she will pronounce you "the most charming of men." You will have shown yourself clever and well-bred. Never seem studied in your phrases, nor talk above the comprehension or contrary to the taste of the person addressed, otherwise you may be voted either a pedant or a bore.

The woman who wishes her conversation to be agreeable will avoid conceit or affectation, and laughter which is not natural and spontaneous. Her language will be easy and unstudied, marked by a graceful carelessness, which, at the same time, never oversteps the limits of propriety. Her lips will readily yield to a pleasant smile; she will not love to hear herself talk; her tones will bear the impress of sincerity, and her eyes kindle with animation, as she speaks. The art of pleasing is, in truth, the very soul of good-breeding; for the precise object of the latter is to render us agreeable to all with whom we associate: to make us, at the same time, esteemed and loved.

We need scarcely advert to the rudeness of interrupting any one who is speaking, or to the impropriety of pushing, to its full extent, a discussion which has become unpleasant.

Some men have a mania for Greek and Latin quotations; this is a peculiarity to be avoided. Nothing is more wearisome than pedantry.

If you feel your intellectual superiority to any one with whom you are conversing, do not seek to bear him down; it would be an inglorious triumph and a breach of good manners. Beware, too, of speaking lightly of subjects which bear a sacred character. No person, man or woman, will think the more of you for irreligious expression.

Witlings occasionally gain a reputation in society; but nothing is more insipid and in worse taste than their conceited harangues and self-sufficient air. Do NOT TRY to be witty. True wit comes spontaneously, and is not forced.

It is a common idea that the art of writing and the art of conversation are one; this is a great mistake. A man of genius may be a very dull talker.

The two grand modes of making conversation interesting, are to enliven it by recitals calculated to affect and impress your hearers, and to intersperse it with anecdotes and agreeable relations.

ADDRESS OF LETTERS, DIRECTIONS FOR WRITING, ETC.

How to Address, and kind of Paper to Use—Seals, Franks, Superscriptions, etc.—The Forms generally Used—On Style—The Proprieties of Language—Praise and Flattery out of Place—Models not always Available—Letters to Friends—A "Dime Letter Writer" in Press,

A letter addressed to a person of eminence should have a seal on the envelope; for other letters the ordinary envelope is sufficient. Letter paper (other than for business) with designs of any kind is in questionable taste, as are seals ornamented with flowers and figures. Perfectly plain paper should be preferred: it may be embossed with the writer's initials. On the birth-days of your relations, and on the festival of the New Year, you can hardly dispense with written congratulations.

In writing to a superior employ paper of full "letter" size; write the name, and in the line underneath the words, "Dear Sir." Leave a line between this word and the first line of your letter. Always write to the point—using not a superfluous or meaningless word, and be as brief as possible. Abbreviations are admissible in notes entered in a book of reference, but not elsewhere, except in commercial correspondence.

Letters of invitation and circulars should always be franked; and if the distance be not too great, they should be sent by hand.

A letter given to a third person, if it be a letter of introduction, should *not* be sealed.

In writing to an official, leave a large margin, for he may need it for marginal notes.

A young man writing to one advanced in years, should not conclude his letter with the common phrase, "Receive, sir, the assurance of my regard." It should be, "Accept, sir, this expression of the regards of your very humble servant."

This formula may be employed in writing to an equal, "Accept, sir, the assurance of my highest esteem;" or, "I have the honor to be yours, very truly."

To a lady, "Accept, madam, the assurance of my respect;" or, "I am, my dear lady, yours very sincerely."

It is ill-bred to write on a half-sheet; the shortest letter requires a whole one.

All letters must be pre-paid. And stamps should *always* be remitted, where an answer is expected, if your own affairs are concerned. Never impose postage upon a friend: it is a contemptible act to make a person, after the trouble of writing to you on your business, pay his own postage.

A few words on epistolary style. Few persons know how to write a good letter. The epistolary style, in general, should be very simple; pathos would be absurd where you have to speak of the common occurrences of life, the follies of the world, its petty hatreds and vanities. Be as respectful and as lively as you can in writing to an old man: old people love sprightliness. The surest way to please in your correspondence is to acquaint yourself with the characters of the persons with whom you interchange letters, to avoid touching their foibles, to speak to them on the subjects they have studied, or of which they are especially fond. In addressing a lady, imply your opinion of her taste by seeking her advice on subjects which require it. Never weary of burning incense; there is an altar in the heart of woman, and even of man, always ready to receive its fragrance. The design of good-breeding is to make you agreeable to every one; write your letters so that each one reading them will be pleased and satisfied. Adulation or flattery is very unbecoming, except it is positively deserved; and then it should be given in terms which will not compromise good taste and good judgment.

If there be a phrase happily worded in the letter addressed to you, ever so little, do not suffer it to fall to the ground; preserve it, and in your reply, show that you have appreciated it.

If a correspondent uses improper language toward you, let your reply be polite, even if it is severe; you will thus inflict a double wound—showing yourself to be a man of dignity, and know how to preserve your self-respect.

Refrain from addressing extravagant praise to a man of discernment; he will see that you have some purpose in what you say, and you will make an enemy. No praise is extravagant to fools; tell them that they are gods, and they will set about procuring an altar; but you would view yourself with contempt if you were mean enough to praise such.

Avoid the folly of copying, *as models*, letters to which peculiar circumstances impart brilliancy or genuine wit; but which, applied from different cases, are strangely out of place.

If you address one beneath you in education or position, don't make him feel his inferiority; be polite without familiarity, as politeness is *due* from every man of good parts to those beneath him.

If you write an epistle respecting a common occurrence in a style of bombast or would-be-eloquence, you will suggest an application to yourself of the fable of the mountain which brought forth a mouse.

In all cases, where it is possible, avoid erasures and crowded lines.

Letters between friends are simply conversation; from an inferior to a superior they should have a tone of caution, at once concise and respectful. A letter of business is expressed in brief and precise terms, with details arranged in exact order. Letters of congratulation should be distinguished for choice language, to the exclusion of all expressions parasitical or common-place. As to the style which a son should employ in writing to his parents, there is no instructor but the heart. In every case and circumstance be truthful and earnest, and you may rest assured you will impress favorably, and accomplish your purpose a thousandfold better than if you used deceitful and false expressions.

The Dime Letter Writer will embody all that is necessary to enable the young person, or the novice, to write letters intelligibly, properly, and satisfactorily. It will contain besides models for hints, a complete directory to correct composition.

BALLS, EVENING-PARTIES, RECEPTIONS, ETC.

Whole Etiquette and Observances of these Occasions, with Special Remarks to both Sexes upon Deportment, Proprieties, etc.—A Chapter for all Young Persons to Read,

To deport oneself satisfactorily at the dance, it is necessary to understand much about the dances which may be introduced. It is a charming accomplishment to be a good dancer, and we shall not hesitate to advise all, male and female, to learn the Terpsichorean art, ere the days of youth are past. It is unnecessary to argue the *pros* and *cons* of the proprieties and moralities of the dance; we prefer to let each judge for him or herself on the debated question; but, that it is a real accomplishment, and a desirable one, to be familiar with the etiquette and technicalities of the ball or soiree, is our most firm conviction, and we therefore introduce such observations and rules here as should govern the occasions of balls, soirees, receptions, etc.

An invitation to a dance should be given at least a week beforehand. A lady sometimes requires time to prepare her toilet. The host of the house receives you; and after the usual compliments, which should be very brief, do not fail in polite recognitions to any lady in the company with whom you are acquainted. If you introduce a friend, make him acquainted with the names of the chief persons present; by this precaution you will often save him an indiscretion; and make him feel more at his ease. These ball-room introductions are *not* regarded as introductions for a more extended acquaintance than for the evening. Should the parties afterward meet upon the street or elsewhere, let the gentleman be careful not to presume upon any recognition of the lady until *she* has *first* bowed. If she fails to extend this recognition, let the gentleman take no umbrage, for he has no real claim upon her acquaintance merely from a public ball-room introduction. An introduction at a *private* soiree is another thing; there the relations of the parties introduced are the same as at any private party: they are *permanently* introduced if at all.

If a gentleman escorts a lady to the dance, he is her cavalier for the evening; he must see that she is always provided with agreeable partners; that she always has a seat when required; has the necessary refreshments, etc. He must dance with her *first* of all, and as often, during the evening, as is proper, considering the claims of others and the wishes of the lady.

Avoid seeking the same partner (other than your lady *en charge*) in the dance too often; you will excite remark, and will expose yourself to the charge of partiality or perhaps of coquetry. It is a graceful attention in a young man to select as partners those ladies whose want of personal attractions condemn them to the terrible punishment of being the "wall-flowers" of the evening. Such attentions will procure you a feeling of grateful regard, especially if you acquit yourself with tact and real kindness.

If a married lady is present, and dancing while her husband is in the room, a person desiring her for a partner should first *be sure* that it is agreeable to the husband for him to offer his hand to the lady.

If a crowd is present, and a gentleman has occasion to make his way through a press of crinoline and drapery, he should proceed most carefully—haste would be very rude and inexcusable; the danger of soiling, or tearing, or disarranging a lady's costume forbids any gentleman making a careless step.

If it is necessary to step in front of a lady in passing, always apologize for the step; otherwise she may very properly think you do not know what belongs to good manners. A lady is always *pleased* with an *apology* if it is gracefully and kindly made; and no gentleman will ever suffer such an occasion to pass in silence, without he really designs an affront, or except he is absolutely ignorant of what is proper and respectful.

A good authority before us says:—In a quadrille, or other dance, while awaiting the music, or while unengaged, a lady and gentleman should avoid long conversations, as they are apt to interfere with the progress of the dance; while, on the other hand, a gentleman should not stand like an automaton, as though he were afraid of his partner, but endeavor to render himself agreeable by those "airy nothings" which amuse for the moment, and are in harmony with the occasion. You should, however, not only on such occasions, but invariably, avoid the use of *slang* terms and phrases, they being, to the last degree, vulgar and objectionable. Indeed, one of the charms of conversation consists in the correct use of language. Dr. Johnson, whose reputation as a *talker* was hardly less than that which he acquired as a writer, prided himself on the appositeness of his quotations, the choice of his words, and the correctness of his expressions. Had he lived in this "age of progress," he would have discovered that his Lexicon was not only incomplete, but required numerous emendations. We can fancy the irritable moralist endeavoring to comprehend the idea which a young lady wishes to convey, when she expresses the opinion that a bonnet is "*awful*," or a young gentleman of his coat, when he asserts that it is "*played out!*" If any one thing marks a person's "bringing up," it is the language used in company; and it may be set down as an almost invariable rule, that any one who uses *slang* words, who talks loudly and rudely, who utters an oath, or who becomes angered and expresses it, is *no* gentleman, and has not had good associations. For a *lady* to be guilty of even one of these sins, is too palpably inexcusable to need remark.

The author quoted above, adds this excellent advice upon a very common ball-room sin, viz.: scandal and strictures upon a person's appearance, dress, etc. He says:—"There is a custom which is sometimes practiced both in the assembly-room and at private parties, which can not be too strongly reprehended,—we allude to the habit of ridicule and ungenerous criticism of those who are ungraceful, or otherwise obnoxious to censure, which is indulged in by the thoughtless, particularly among the dancers. Of its gross impropriety and vulgarity we need hardly express an opinion; but there is such an utter disregard for the feelings of others implied in this kind of negative censorship, that we can not forbear to warn our young readers to avoid it. The 'Koran' says: 'Do not mock—the mocked may be better than the mocker.' Those you condemn may not have had the same advantages as yourself in acquiring grace or dignity, while they may be infinitely superior in purity of heart and mental accomplishments. The advice of Chesterfield to his son, in his commerce with society, to *do as you would be done by*, is founded on the Christian precept, and worthy of commendation. Imagine yourself the victim of others' ridicule, and you will cease to indulge in a pastime which only gains for you the hatred of those you satirize, if they chance to observe you, and the contempt of others who have noticed your violation of politeness, and abuse of true sociality."

Ladies will always be careful of their associates. At the public ball are occasionally to be found persons whose acquaintance it is not proper to make. The young female is ever the cynosure of all eyes, and can not comport herself too strictly, nor choose her partners too carefully. It is not best to be "prudish," but it is right and necessary to be cautious and discreet.

In walking up or down the room the lady should always be accompanied by a gentleman; it is quite improper to saunter around alone.

When a young lady declines dancing with a gentleman, it is her duty to give him a reason why, although some thoughtless ones do not. No matter how frivolous it may be, it is simply an act of courtesy to offer him an excuse; while, on the other hand, no gentleman ought so far to compromise his self-respect as to take the slightest offence at seeing a lady by whom he has just been refused, dance immediately after with some one else. A lady has a hundred motives for conduct which she can not explain; and for a gentleman to take offence at her simple declination to dance is very silly and unmanly.

During the act of dancing all parties should have on their summer looks. Dancing is rightly supposed to be an *enjoyment*, but the somber countenances of some who engage in it, might almost lead to the belief that it were a solemn duty being performed. If, says a shrewd observer, those who laugh in church would transfer their merriment to the assembly-room, and those who are sad in the assembly-room would carry their gravity to the church, they both might discover the appositeness of Solomon's declaration, that "there is a time to be merry and a time to be sad."

It should ever be the study of both sexes to render themselves agreeable. Gentlemen, as we have said, should avoid showing *marked* preference to particular ladies, by devoting their undivided attentions to them, or dancing exclusively with them. Too often, the "belle of the evening," with no other charms than beauty of form and feature, monopolizes the regards of a circle of admirers, while modest merit, of less personal attraction, is both overlooked and neglected. We honor the generous conduct of those, particularly the "well-favored," who bestow their attentions on ladies who, from conscious lack of beauty, least expect them. The real man of sense will not fail to recognize most solicitously any lady who may seem neglected or unattended.

On the other hand, no lady, however numerous the solicitations of her admirers, should consent to dance repeatedly when, by so doing, she excludes other ladies from participating in the same amusement; still less, as we have hinted, should she dance exclusively with the same gentleman, to the disadvantage of others.

What has elsewhere been said in regard to dress and ornament will apply fully to the occasion of the dance. Let *simplicity* be the guide, and not display. The lady tricked out in many jewels and ribbons looks too much like a moving advertisement to command respect for it. If ladies generally knew how deep an impression a pure style of dress makes upon the other sex, and realized how trifling a gaudy dress seems to the person of true taste, we surmise their vanity alone would impel to simpler attire, rather than to elaborate and costly display.

In regard to a gentleman's dress for the dance, we may add: white gloves, white vest, light colored cravat, dress-coat, black pants, and patent-leather gaiters, or light calf-skin boots well polished, constitute the proper ball-room or soiree costume. The much talked of "independence" of Americans, professes disdain of many of the requisitions of dress established by good usage in England and France. A *frock*-coat would not be tolerated a moment in any fashionable society in Europe. Whether it be esteemed a prejudice or otherwise, we are free to confess that, in our own opinion, the frock-coat is a violation of good taste, as unsuited either to a ball-room or private assembly. The ordinary dress-coat, which is in no respect in the way, and which leaves the limbs perfectly free to move gracefully, is the only proper coat for the party and dance.

When a lady has accepted refreshment, her attending gentleman should hasten to relieve her of her glass or plate; and, as her cavalier, should see that all her wants and wishes have been complied with. The refreshments over, the gentleman should offer his arm and gallant the lady to her seat in the ball-room; or, if she wishes to retire to the dress-room, he should gallant her to the door, and there await her coming out to convey her to the dancing-floor again. The ladies dressing-room, it is unnecessary to say, is a sacred precinct into which no man should ever presume to look; to go into it would be an outrage which none could overlook or forgive.

When the hour comes for retiring home, be sure to be ready for the lady whom you have accompanied to the dance; your obligations are not discharged until she is again, under your own eyes, seen safely at her own door. If you have come to the room unattended, select, during the latter part of the evening, some lady who, it may seem, will be glad of your company home; offer her your services and, if she signifies assent, be careful to be ready at her call. Await at the door of the dressing-room for her, and offering your arm do the gallant kindly but not ostentatiously nor too officiously. Leave her at her own door, after the bell has been answered, and not until then.

In leaving an evening-party it is unnecessary to seek the master of the house. Your farewell will be dispensed with; you should leave without disturbing any one to occasion remark. This rule is often misunderstood, but it should not be.

THE CARD AND CHESS TABLE, ETC.

Etiquette of Sociable Games—Chess and its Proprieties—Cheerfulness a Necessary Companion for all Players,

It is well at a ball, to have a table for cards and men for chess: for all the guests are not dancers, and it is the duty of a host to see that *all* enjoy themselves. It is customary for partners to bow slightly to each other before beginning a game of cards or chess. When a game of cards is ended, and the "shuffle" is your partner's, the cards should be arranged and handed to the lady whose turn it is to deal them.

To discuss the rules of play is ungenteel. In a quiet party the tact and cordiality of the entertainers should put all the guests at their ease.

The choice of the guests is not one of the least difficult points. At the house of a political man, there should be an effort to unite all shades of opinion. From parties of any kind, a man known for his gratuitous rudeness, or for the impropriety of his witticism, will be excluded by all who are desirous of maintaining the proprieties of social intercourse. Opposing politicians, editors, lawyers, and ministers should *never* carry their *professional* feelings into the parlor, nor, by any expression, mar the good-humor of an evening.

It is improper to express your opinion loudly in company, or to remain long at the card-table when you are young and known to be a good dancer.

It is a delicate attention to stand behind a lady at the piano and turn over the leaves of her music-book, and after the music to gallant her to her seat. After the dance, a gentleman must not omit to conduct his partner to her seat; and in so doing, a well-turned compliment will not be out of place.

We have noted the impropriety of a young man's remaining long at the chess or the card table, when the ladies are in want of a partner in the adjoining room. At the same time, a gentleman should be acquainted with one or more games, as it is polite to play with the host or his guests, if you are invited to do so.

Some persons, in playing cards, show an effort to conceal their hand; this is ill-bred. If it be a pleasure to spectators to watch the game, why should you object to it? Even if it be disagreeable to you to be overlooked, you should not let it appear.

You will sometimes see one partner reproach another sharply for unskillful play; thus convicting himself of being more unskilled in the science of good-breeding.

The man who utters noisy complaints about his luck, or manifests unseemly joy at winning a game, raising his voice to a high key on all occasions, is so ignorant as to be unworthy of admission into a drawing-room.

In playing chess, avoid the other extreme of being too silent and abstracted, for such conduct is only fit for the study.

Use a cheerful air, and make others feel your geniality, if you would win hearts as well as games.

ENTERTAINMENTS, DINNER-PARTIES, ETC.

The whole Etiquette of such Occasions, including General and Special Directions

"To give an invitation," says a brilliant writer, "is to take the responsibility of your guest's happiness during the time he is under your roof." This is an ambitious view of the subject; we will alter it thus: "To invite a man, is to undertake to do all in your power to make him feel satisfied with the pleasure you offer him." In order to do which, it is essential to know the tastes of your guests. To invite two persons at enmity with each other, to an entertainment, is a blunder; it is unpardonable to bring such together in a small party, unless, indeed, the way to reconciliation lies open; and even in this case there is an awkwardness in the presence of enemies, which will not fail to render their presence unpleasant to others.

"The pleasures of the table," says the author of the "Physiology of Taste," "belong to all ages, to all ranks, to all countries; they may be enjoyed with all other pleasures, and remain the longest to console us for their loss." That this enjoyment may be undisturbed, take care that nothing occurs to chagrin any of the guests; if, therefore, the conversation falls upon a subject disagreeable to any one present, good-breeding requires that the host should skillfully turn it upon another topic.

An invitation to dinner should be given at least two days beforehand, except in extraordinary cases. From an inferior to a superior, it should be made in person.

In ceremonious dinners, the place of each guest is assigned beforehand; you thus avoid putting several ladies together. Each one should have a gentleman next her.

The host offers his arm to the lady deserving of most consideration. Young people should yield to those more advanced in years. Do not forget, in passing the threshold of a door, to *precede* the lady who leans on your arm. This is an exception to the general rule; in every other case, the gentleman should retire a step, to allow the lady to pass.

Before passing into the dining-room, each gentleman offers his *left* arm to a lady, and conducts her to table.

Beware of arriving too early or too late: in either case there is an awkwardness—in the former you inconvenience your host; in the latter, his guests.

Once at table, you should not lose sight of the plate or glass of your fair neighbor, showing yourself attentive, without affectation or over-officiousness.

Meat should be cut only according as it is carried to the mouth. To cut up a plateful is the very height of greediness and ill-breeding.

Bread is broken as it is wanted; after soup, which is served out by the host, the spoon remains on the plate, as it will not be used again.

Where wine is used, three glasses are usually laid down to each guest at dinner: one for ordinary wines; another of smaller size for claret; the third to receive the sparkling foam of the champagne. In drinking you should say to your neighbor, "Sir, may I offer you?" and not employ the ungenteel phrase, "Will you take?" as if you were at the bar of some ordinary drinking-saloon.

If the dish that you desire be too far from your neighbor, do not ask another guest; the servant will attend your orders.

The noise of the knife and plate should be heard as little as possible; rapidity in eating is also ill-bred.

A knowledge of carving is indispensable to all men who would act the host with grace and propriety.

Do not assist yourself to any dish where servants stand ready to supply you.

Some persons use their bread at dinner to dry up their plates; this is intolerable beyond the family circle, and even there is rather childish.

Parents should be careful to save their children from awkwardness in company, either in treading on a lady's dress, or using the knife in eating; or worse still, their fingers.

Never take any thing out of your pocket to lay on the table.

The napkin should rest on the knees, only half unfolded. The fork is never to be laid on its back.

The host has the knives changed for dessert.

The knife and fork, and the table utensils generally should never be handed endways, but should be held by the middle.

Coffee is generally served after passing into the drawing room. The lady of the house fills it out if it be after dinner; after breakfast this office may be left to a servant.

The hostess should not seek to outvie her guests in the costliness of her toilet. This would be in bad taste.

In England, it is the custom for ladies to retire a little before the close of the meal. American ladies are not disposed to admire this habit, and we are too gallant and too anxious to enjoy the charm of their conversation, to subject them to this mode of banishment.

The lady of the house should show the same solicitude for all her guests, and take care that they want for nothing.

In some houses, a custom has been adopted, which appears to us vulgar, viz: the gentlemen retire from the company for a short time *to smoke*; on their return to the ladies, their clothes and breath exhale the disagreeable perfume. There are few well-bred women to whom tobacco is not extremely offensive.

The host rises to leave the table; you must remember not to fold your napkin, as is usual in the family, where the same napkin serves you several times. Each gentleman offers his arm to a lady, and conducts her back to the drawing-room.

The Romans knew how to enhance, by enjoyments unknown to us, the pleasures of the table; and the Greeks threw more poetry into their festivals than our somewhat prosaic eaters. At the banquets of Greece, the sculptured cups were crowned with roses; singers and musicians enlivened the close of the repast; and the wit of the professed jester contributed to the entertainment of the guests.

The table and side-board and mantels will always look more inviting when dressed tastefully in flowers. A sweet bouquet before each lady is a personal compliment which it is easy to bestow, and one which can not fail to please the guests.

ETIQUETTE OF THE STREET.

Explicit Directions for Behavior on the Street—A True Gentleman known by his Demeanor—How to Treat Ladies

Good behavior upon the street, or public promenade, marks the gentleman most effectually; rudeness, incivility, disregard of "what the world says," marks the person of low breeding. We always know, in walking a square with a man, if he is a gentleman or not. A real gentility never does the following things on the street, in presence of observers:—

Never picks the teeth, nor scratches the head.

Never swears or talks uproariously.

Never picks the nose with the finger.

Never smokes, or spits upon the walk, to the exceeding annoyance of those who are always disgusted with tobacco in any shape.

Never stares at any one, man or woman, in a marked manner.

Never scans a lady's dress impertinently, and makes no rude remarks about her.

Never crowds before promenaders in a rough or hurried way.

Never jostles a lady or gentleman without an "excuse me."

Never treads upon a lady's dress without begging pardon.

Never loses temper, nor attracts attention by excited conversation.

Never dresses in an odd or singular manner, so as to create remark.

Never fails to raise his hat politely to a lady acquaintance; nor to a male friend who may be walking with a lady—it is a courtesy to the lady.

Of course a lady will not be rude, nor dress so as attract undue attention, much less to create unpleasant remark. She will be kind to all; she will not absorb too much of the walk, nor fail to give half the way to either a lady or gentleman; she will not allow her skirts to drag upon the walk to the annoyance of other pedestrians; she will not fail to recognize friends by a pleasant smile and slight bow; she will not look back at any one who has passed her; she will not eye another lady's dress, as if studying its very texture; she will not stop upon the walk to talk with a friend to the inconvenience of others; she will not make the street a place of meeting with a person whom she can not receive at her house. Some females do, it is true, not regard all these laws of proper and recognized etiquette; and such, we are forced to say, forfeit their claim to be called a lady. A true lady in the street, as in the parlor or *salon*, is modest, discreet, kind, obliging; if she is to the contrary, she forfeits her right to be called after the truly genteel.

It is a most unfailing mark of ignorance and low origin to "put on airs," and to show pride, vanity, egotism in the street. The truly well-educated, well-born, and well-bred *never* betray vanity, conceit, superciliousness, nor hauteur. Set this down as an invariable law, and, male or female, let it guide all your actions.

It is proper that the lady should *first* recognize the gentleman. There has been some dispute on this point of etiquette, but we think there can be no question of the propriety of the first recognition coming from the lady. A gentleman will never fail to bow in return to a lady, even if he may feel coldly disposed toward her; but a lady may not feel at liberty to return a gentleman's bow, which places him in a rather unpleasant position. A lady should give the first smile or bow, is the rule now recognized.

In meeting acquaintances several times during the same promenade, it is not necessary to salute them at every passing.

In offering a lady your arm, as it is proper to do upon the street, particularly in the evening, always give her the *right* arm, because persons in passing, observing the law "turn to the right," would jostle her if she was upon the left arm. The practice of always giving the lady the inside of the walk, is a very useless one, and not necessary to true politeness.

It is always proper for a gentleman walking alone, or with another of his sex, to give the lady, or a gentleman with a lady, the inside of the walk.

In gallanting a lady to a carriage, take her left hand. It is truly polite to take off the hat in such a service.

THE POLITENESS OF BUSINESS.

How Proper Politeness is, in Employees and Employers—Rules which should Invariably Mark their Deportment

A volume might with propriety be written on business proprieties, for the rules of good-breeding are so outrageously violated by employees and employers, that to detail their shortcomings would require many pages. But in business as in all other intercourse, the one invariable law of good-breeding, viz.: kindness, offers the key to all true mode of conduct. Be kind and considerate, and you will do right.

The upright and model man of business never commits any of the following sins:—

Never tells a falsehood, even though at times it may offer a temporary advantage. In the end it will not result happily—neither to conscience nor to the till. It is one of the fixed laws of compensations that a wrong entails evil, sooner or later; hence, even in a selfish view, it is best always to tell the truth.

Never creates false expectations to effect a transaction.

Never represents an article to be what it is not. The secret of the success of A. T. Stewart, and other merchants of eminence, is that they never would allow any deception to be practiced upon customers. A child can buy of them as safely as an experienced person.

Never breaks appointments, and never fails to keep good his word to the hour and the letter, if there is no just cause to prevent.

Never is absent from his business, except when absolutely necessary.

Never allows others in his employ to do what is not perfectly intelligible to him. Always understands his books; always keeps the run of the entire day's transactions; always knows the exact state of his bank account; always is acquainted with the doings of each one in his employ.

If called upon by any person he is polite; he gives no curt answers; he keeps none waiting unnecessarily; he is solicitous of doing what will most please.

In a word, the secret of business success, and the true criterion of action for the business man, young or old, is to be found in that blessed Golden Rule, which will forever hold good, viz.:—

Do unto others as ye would that they should do unto you.

ADVICE TO THE WORKING-MAN.

Politeness Essential to all—Boorishness Intolerable and Injurious—The true Relation between the various Workers in Society,

Let it not be said that the first principles of good breeding are unknown to the working-man; he may be ignorant of the usages of society, but he can, if he please, maintain a becoming and agreeable deportment. What generally makes him coarse and surly, is the prejudice, unhappily too widely spread, that the rich man feels above him. This is a great mistake; it is not the blouse that is shunned, it is the rudeness of the man who wears it. Labor is always held in esteem by any man of sense; but who can regard coarseness and rudeness with respect? Two workmen enter a saloon, they talk as if in the street, abuse those whom they name "aristocrats," and make such a disturbance, that the waiter shows them to the door. Is it the working-man who is thus used? no, verily, it is the insulter of the public. A man in broadcloth, who should conduct himself thus, would, in like manner, be requested to retire from the company of those whom he was disturbing. However, the operative thus treated, always exclaims: "Though one is a workman, he is as good as you." But, in this case, he is not in the character of a working-man, but in that of a consumer, like all the others seeking their comfort or pleasure; none of whom would think of saying, if such a thing happened to them, "I am a lawyer;" or, "I am a physician;" or, "I am an officer." In a public establishment, such as a *cafe*, or hotel, or in public conveyances, all are equal, and no one should be suffered to be insolent, or vulgar, or rude.

The rich man, on his part, knows that there are laws of politeness to be observed toward all. The upstart or snob alone gives himself the habit of speaking rudely to those he employs; he alone affects to humble them by his tone of superiority. The man of *true* nobility is polite to every one, be he rich or poor.

LOVE, COURTSHIP, AND MARRIAGE.[1]

A Chapter by an Eminent Author—The Language of True Love and its Expression—The True Relations of the Sexes—Coquetry and Flirting a Mark of Baseness—Courtship—Its Modes of Procedure and its Proper Manifestation—Its Attendant Responsibilities—Marriage—The Solemn Character of the Occasion—Its Forms of Procedure, and Rites of the Ceremony—After-Marriage Customs and Observances

In the matter of LOVE it would be hard to lay down any formal rules; the heart is its own teacher; if *its* impulses be true and pure, your looks, words, and actions will be in no danger of doing you any particular discredit. Even awkwardness is sometimes eloquent, and makes a better companion than the most elegant self-possession, since it proclaims the reality of your passion, and the diffidence of real affection. Love has a language of its own, and will not thank any book of etiquette for a lesson. If the maiden be modest, and the youth sincere and manly, they will appreciate and understand each other without danger of mistakes.

It has been said that any refined and delicate woman can *prevent* an offer which she does not intend to accept, and we believe that, in most cases, she can; saving herself the pain of refusal, and her lover the mortification of being rejected.

It is a poor triumph for a young lady to say, or to feel, that she has refused five, ten, or twenty offers of marriage; it is about the same as acknowledging herself a trifler and coquette, who, from motives of personal vanity, tempts and induces hopes and expectations which she has predetermined shall be disappointed. Such a course is, to a certain degree, both unprincipled and immodest.

It is a still greater crime when a man conveys the impression that he is in love, by actions, gallantries, looks, attentions, all—except that he never commits himself—and finally withdraws his devotions, exulting in the thought that he has said or written nothing which can legally bind him.

[1] There is much preposterous stuff before the public, in the way of books relating to love and its relations, to marriage, and to wedded life. We look upon these works, as a general thing, as vicious in their nature, because they excite passions and feelings and expectations of which no one needs to be specially informed; while their detail of processes necessary to accomplish a wished for "happy result" are truly disgusting. A person's own heart, and the advice of some good sensible married friend, are all sufficient for the necessary guidance of a man or woman designing marriage. We propose, in some future work, to introduce this matter more fully to our readers, in a series of papers especially addressed to young and to married folks. We here give such general rules and observances as seem proper to be adverted to in a work on etiquette.

But true love, as we remarked before, will find for itself some becoming expression and —

"needs not the foreign child of ornament."

Love, of course, unless some insuperable barrier exists, will be followed in due time by Courtship. Here some formalities will begin to be observed. The passion which blushed to own itself to itself, having been crowned, becomes a matter of interest to others than the two most particularly concerned. If a young man thinks fit to address himself *first* to the young lady, to find if his attentions be agreeable to her, he should not delay, after gaining her consent to them, to respectfully solicit the approval of her parents or guardians. This is due to them, and should not be put off on account of any unworthy fear or timidity.

It is customary in some circles for the parents to make the betrothal immediately known to their friends, and even to give a kind of preliminary festival at which the couple are publicly congratulated.

Good taste will dictate the avoidance of any expression of fondness between the parties when in company.

Envy and satire are ever on the look-out for subjects of ridicule, and it is well to give them no opportunity. Sentiment which is beautiful in the family circle, is often odious in society. The same rule holds good with relatives and newly-married people. Their devotion to each other should be put aside, and the claims of others upon their courtesy and time duly honored.

The amount of attention permissible before marriage, such as walking, driving, concert-going, etc., depends very much upon the customs of the place in which the persons reside. Public opinion and habit should not be invaded without some good and weighty reason, even with the most innocent purposes. It can not be desirable to provoke remark and censure, however indifferent you may feel towards its authors.

The Marriage ceremony varies with the fortunes and wishes of those interested.

In regard to the form of the rite, no specific direction are necessary; for those who are to be married by ministers, will study the form of their particular church — the Methodists their "Book of Discipline," the Episcopalians their "Book of Common Prayer," the Catholics their Ritual, etc., etc. In most cases a rehearsal of the ceremony is made in private, that the pair may the more perfectly understand the necessary forms. If the parties are to be wedded by a magistrate, the ceremony is almost nominal — it is a mere repetition of a vow. The Catholic and Episcopal forms have the most ceremony, and doubtless are the most impressive, though no more effectually marrying than the simplest form.

There are, however, some generally received rules which govern this momentous and interesting occasion, and to these we refer all interested.

When the wedding is not strictly in private, it is customary for bridesmaids and groomsmen to be chosen to assist in the duties of the occasion.

The bridesmaids should be *younger* than the bride; their dresses should be *conformed to hers*; they should not be any more expensive, though they are permitted more ornament. They are generally chosen of light, graceful material; flowers are the principal decoration.

The bride's dress is marked by simplicity. But few jewels or ornaments should be worn, and those should be the gift of the bridegroom or parents. A veil and garland are the distinguishing features of the dress.

The bridesmaids assist in dressing the bride, receiving the company, etc.; and, at the time of the ceremony, stand at her *left* side, the first bridesmaid holding the bouquet and gloves.

The groomsmen receive the clergyman, present him to the couple to be married, and support the bridegroom upon the *right*, during the ceremony.

If it is an evening wedding, at home, immediately after "these twain are made one," they are congratulated: first by the relatives, then by the friends, receiving the good wishes of all; after which, they are at liberty to leave their formal position, and mingle with the company. The dresses, supper, etc., are usually more festive and gay than for a morning wedding and reception, where the friends stop for a few moments only, to congratulate the newly-married pair, taste the cake and wine, and hurry away.

When the ceremony is performed in church, the bride enters at the *left*, with her father, mother, and bridesmaids; or, at all events, with a bridesmaid. The groom enters at the *right*, followed by his attendants. The parents stand behind, the attendants at either side.

The bride should be certain that her glove is readily removable; the groom, that the ring is where he can find it, to avoid delay and embarrassment.

When they leave the church, the newly-married couple walk arm-in-arm. They have usually a reception of a couple of hours at home, for their intimate friends, then a breakfast, then leave upon the "bridal tour."

The wording of invitations, and the styles of cards, are so constantly changing, that it will not do to lay down rules. Cards of invitation *to* the wedding are usually sent out in the *name of the mother*. [See page 70.]

A few days before the return of the wedded pair, their own especial card is sent to those whom they desire shall call upon them, and whose acquaintance they wish to retain.

However plain the dress chosen for the occasion, gloves and shoes must be faultless. There should be flowers if possible; they are never more in place.

The fee of the clergyman will be decided by the fortune and position of the groom. No doubt, in the joy of his heart, the just married will be liberal; if he is not, upon *this* occasion, he never will be. The *first groomsman* will take charge of this matter.

The travelling dresses should not be marked by "bridal favors," if the happy couple wish to avoid the curious scrutiny of strangers.

Married people should never intrude "family jars" nor family devotion upon company. Husband and wife should be pleasant and affectionate in their demeanor, with a show of reserve, while in the presence of "the world." It is improper to say "husband" and "wife," in speaking of your companion to others. Use their title, as Mr. or Mrs.—that is, to all but intimate friends. Especially, do not introduce, "my wife," or "my husband." Caresses, disagreements, and significant glances betraying secret intelligence, are all out of place in general company.

The "honeymoon" is a mythic time. It is generally regarded as extending to the first six weeks, during which period the young couple must give themselves up to receptions of friends, to attending parties made in their honor, etc. The real honeymoon *should* last *through life*, and will, if the pair is properly mated. Therefore, let the choice be made in no haste and passion and blindness, but in deliberation and calm exercise of judgment.

RESPECT FOR RELIGION AND FOR OLD AGE.

Remarks Designed for the Young of both Sexes, and Advice they will not Fail to Profit by

Some young people seem to imagine that they are living in the age of Voltaire, and make a merit of skeptical and even atheistical opinions. They laugh at the sacred character of the ministry, and deride what is venerable and sacred. This class is as deserving of contempt, as it is avoided in truly good society. Impiety is no longer fashionable as it was in the days when an atheistical philosopher thought to make laws for the world, and construe liberty into license to outrage every pious instinct.

A man who does not respect the religion of his fathers, is incapable of knowing, and therefore of applying, the laws of good-breeding. A young man who boasts his freedom of religious opinions, is but confessing his own ignorance, for his belief is, in most cases, the result of a perfect non-acquaintance with religious systems. How many of our boasted "free thinkers" are men of pure lives and noble instincts?

Another sin is its want of respect for women and for persons of advanced years. A man of religious feeling holds himself bound to those duties, in respect to old age, that were observed in ancient times. But the young men of whom we have been speaking make a parade of rudeness in the presence of an old man; they pay him no more respect than if he were an unfledged youth of eighteen like themselves; they smoke cigars under his nose; scarcely deign to acknowledge him in the street; and never are willing to remember that their father is or was an old man, and that they will themselves grow old. Such respect neither their parents nor themselves. Diogenes declared himself to be a dog that he might have a right to indulge his cynical disposition. So are these flippant theologians who have sunk to the same level.

One word as to the influence of religion upon the character of the young girl. A religious course of training can alone impart to the feminine character that spirit of yielding gentleness which, in domestic, as in public life, is the basis of politeness. Deprived of these qualities, a woman would be unamiable in the family circle, as well as in the world, where, in spite of her efforts to appear pleasing, her bad education would inevitably display itself. Young ladies of this class, if they do not go the length of impertinence, have a dissatisfied air, and indulge in the habit of criticising every thing with severity. If married, they quickly banish peace from the conjugal roof, by their exactions and ill-humor. They are not willing to make a single sacrifice for their husband's happiness; quarrels and oppositions please them, and the gentlest yoke becomes a heavy chain. The husband thus situated may consider himself happy, if his wife will condescend to occupy herself at all with domestic affairs, and things so common as the concerns of the family. An irreligious woman is as much to be abhorred as a drunken woman: she is no longer fit to lead in society and to give tone to its morals; she is not fit to be a mother; for her children will surely be reckless and godless; she is not a grace, but a blot on her sex, disliked even by men who profess to no religious conviction.

SPECIAL WORD, FOR LADIES ONLY.

The Necessities of Particular Styles of Dress—Velvets, Muslins, Complexion, etc.—A fair Face should be Always in Smiles,

What is becoming to one woman, may be just the reverse to another, and in such a case it is foolish to be the slave of fashion. A tall, elegant, and well-formed figure requires a material that will exhibit and set off to advantage these charms.

Velvet suits well a commanding figure which disdains light materials, pale colors, and trifling ornaments. In vain will a new fashion proffer its pretty trinkets: the woman who possesses this classical figure will disdain all such trifles. Her style of head-dress will be chaste; diamond ornaments will sparkle on her bosom; she is a queen, and should wear the ornaments of royalty, provided she can do so.

A young girl, all grace and elegance, will robe her sylph-like form in the most transparent of textures; she will place a fresh garland on her charming brow. Every thing in her dress should correspond to the freshness of her smile, to the sweetness of her expression.

We must, moreover, counsel our fair friends not to spoil their beauty by any act of their own. To explain ourselves further:

We will suppose you to possess a beautiful face, and you have every interest in preserving its regularity. Now mark: If you experience the slightest opposition, your features are not recognizable your forehead is wrinkled, you are ten years older!

Are you angry? your nose contracts, your upper lip is elongated, your eyes are half covered by their lids; you are frightfully ugly!

Are you afraid? your eyebrows are raised, your mouth is half open, and you look like a simpleton!

Are you cold? all your features are contracted, every muscle of your face is in a state of tension, your neck sinks between your shoulders, you are hunch-backed; consequently the blood, less active in this semi-circular position, makes you still colder than if you walked on boldly, and you have further the advantage of looking like a little old man!

Are you negligent in your dress, careless in your habits, idle and listless? your face gradually assumes an expression of creticism, which makes your eyes lose all their vivacity, and your countenance its charms!

Consult your mirror when you experience one of these feelings, and you will hardly recognize yourself.

Since God has given you an agreeable countenance, do not deface his work—all the world will be gainers and yourself also.

Alas! what shall we say to those who have not been favored with a charming countenance? In such a case there is almost always a compensation of Nature's own providing. You will observe that with unprepossessing features, there is generally an elegant figure, or a great deal of expression, or lively wit, that makes you forget that Nature has been less bountiful than is her wont.

Fanciful modes of dress suit the coquette; she knows how to make use of them: they are her counters. She has the art of arranging tastefully even the folds of her dress. Her costume should be full of variety, to be the reflection of her caprices.

CONFIDENTIAL ADVICE TO YOUNG MEN.

**The Great, Invariable Law of Compensations—The True Principles
of Conduct, the and grand Secret of Success,**

We have given such specific directions as have seemed to us necessary to form the gentleman. In many cases it has been necessary to repeat admonitions in order to impress on the mind of the reader the propriety of certain special observances. Let this excuse what may, at times, appear to be a repetition or a tautology. In this chapter we wish to address young men confidentially and candidly upon some of those habits and ways of life which serve to mold the character of the man to a considerable degree, and, hence, are of vital importance in their relations to society and to individuals.

A young man who starts out in life without any settled purpose in mind, is laboring at great disadvantage. He will waste several years in useless and aimless endeavor to "get along," which he ought to have given up to settling and systematizing his life-occupation. If he is to learn a trade, let him resolve upon it at as early a moment as is practicable, and once resolved upon, let all his energies be devoted to his pursuit. Success will be sure to follow such an endeavor; and the age of twenty-five will, beyond a doubt, if health does not fail, find the young man a respected member of community, an efficient workman earning a liberal living, and well qualified to enter upon the business and responsibilities of wedded life. If, on the contrary, the young man allows his majority to find him still deficient in a knowledge of the trade he knows he must or ought to follow, it is almost a moral certainty that he never will attain to the efficiency, the industry, and self-reliance which, otherwise, must have marked him. Learn your trade, then, ere your majority comes; and, when once learned, remember that,

> Through long days of labor,
> And nights devoid of ease,

spring those blessings and rewards which almost inevitably follow upon endeavor rightly directed.

If you propose a commercial life, let there be no hesitation in the decision; but go at it bravely, cheerfully, persistently, that your majority may find you enjoying the confidence of employers, and on the high-road to your own independence. Remember, solemnly remember, that incorruptible honesty, integrity unimpeachable, virtue uncontaminated, are the best riches the *heart* of man can ever attain— that wealth gained at a sacrifice of any of these qualities is a leprosy of gold which will cover the very soul with loathsomeness. If the author of this chapter had a million of dollars to bestow, it would be joyfully hurled into the sea, to be lost forever, if its possessorship could impair the virtue and moral excellence of its recipients. View wealth, as honorable only when honorably attained and rationally enjoyed; and your life will be one which you, your friends, and your children will call blessed.

If you design a professional life, it should be determined on before the years of school-life are ended, that you may direct your studies and mold your thoughts into the most effective channels. As in a commercial life, remember that the keystone of success lies in your honesty. A man who enters upon the practice of the law, or of medicine merely for gain, is starting out with a bad principle, which will not fail to produce bad results even though wealth be obtained; for, if purity of heart, disinterestedness, self-respect are all gone, of what avail is *money*? The veriest vagrant, who comes honestly by his poverty, is a nobler being than he who comes dishonorably by his wealth.

As has been said, in previous pages, gentility has much to do with success in life. It opens a way for progress where no rudeness would avail—it unlocks sympathies, awakens friendships, commands confidences which are better than mortgages and bonds in our dealings with men; and we therefore commend earnestly to your attention what we have said on previous pages in regard to the rules and observances of the good-breeding which indicates true gentility.

CULTIVATE A TASTE FOR THE BEAUTIFUL.

That "the Beautiful" is—Its great Utility in Modifying our Tastes and in Directing our Habits—Art, Music, Books, Female Companionship, all to be Cultivated Sedulously,

What is "the beautiful?" It is what beautifies and graces life. It is the antithesis of the real and practical. It is the glory of life, for it elevates the heart and mind into the contemplation of, and sympathy with, the ideal—the spiritual. Its language is the language of emotion; it startles, and thrills, and stirs within us divine impulses. It comforts life, as the shower comforts the parched grass; and penetrates into the very recesses of our being, as the juices and fluids penetrate the arteries and pores of the plant.

There is so much practicality in our American life, that we are in danger of growing sordid, covetous, unsympathetic, unpoetical; and our lives threaten to be as barren of beauty as the pile of unhewn marble, out of which the glorious edifice *can* be built, if only the hand of the master touches it, and molds it into forms of unity and grace. We want the hand of that master to seize our being, to give it symmetry, to develop its latent glories, to prove its power for developing a fair humanity. The Master already is at the door!

In the cultivation of a taste for music, flowers, and home ornamentation, for art and poetry, for female purity and spiritual grace, we find the means of a right development. These are the messengers of the beautiful, and by their guidance we approach the true shrine.

It is one of the most cheering signs of our civilization, that a taste for music and art is fast spreading among all classes of the American people. Pictures and books are now found in houses where, a few years since, they were utter strangers, and their introduction has caused such a delightful change! That once hard repulsive room is now pleasant, and grace sits at the door. What has wrought the change. A picture or two on the walls, a carpet on the bare floor, a fine book upon the table—these are the secret of the new order which reigns there. And as the taste for these things expands, there will be still more beauty around that house. Vines will creep over the door, the yard will be turned into form and shape, a piano will enter over the door-sill, and "send its wild echoes flying" through all the rooms to make hearts beat with new emotions. Then must follow that intelligence which has the truest appreciation of life, which sees something else in existence than the mere necessities of subsistence, which finds in nature a language before dead, or unmeaning.

A young man should lend himself to think and talk of art, of music, etc., etc.; should visit picture galleries and libraries; should attend good lectures and good concerts, and thus to acquire a taste for such recreation, to fill his mind with good thoughts, and to start in his soul noble aspirations. He who pursues this course, and leaves to others the bar-room, the billiard-room, the race-course, the club-room, is as sure of a high reward, as that intellect and virtue are above mere physical enjoyment and grossness.

Without doubt, the worst enemy of the young man is the drinking and smoking saloon. While we make no pretensions to total abstinence in the use of spirits, we still believe, from a long experience and close observation, that a bar-room resort is that fatal "first step," which starts the career of dissipation, debauchery, and crime. The associations one meets there, the whole moral atmosphere and presence, are deadening to right principles, destructive of right impressions. Beware of them, O young man, is the earnest admonition we have to give to him who peruses this little chapter.

A good antidote to the bad habit of frequenting these too-common places of resort, is to seek the society of intelligent, virtuous females; to go out with them, to sing with them, read with them, talk with them. A true woman's influence is ennobling, and she truly is the director of our race, if we but allow her her real rights to our devotion and our trust.

ETIQUETTE OF HORSEBACK RIDING.

The Uses of this Noble Exercise—The Rules of the Road and the Proper Attentions to Offer—The Dress, etc.

The very delightful recreation and exercise of riding on horseback is too little partaken of in these days of fast locomotion. This is to be regretted, for nothing is better calculated to develop the physical health and animal spirits, nothing is more conducive to pleasure of a rational character, than the ride on horseback upon every pleasant day.

The etiquette of such occasions is simple enough. The lady should have the left, that the skirt may be outside and not interfered with. The gentleman should never be in *advance* of the lady, but always a little in the rear, yet constantly near enough for any emergency, or for a chat. The ceremony of mounting and dismounting is to be learned by practice; no etiquette can teach it. It is, of course, the gentleman's place to gallant the lady out, taking her by her left hand, as, with her right, she must support her skirt; he must assist her to mount by holding the stirrup for her foot, and by disposing of her skirt after she is seated.

The dress of the lady, upon such occasions, is not well understood, by most of our ladies. The English women ride very much, both alone and accompanied, on horseback; sometimes even participating in the exciting and daring race of the hunt. Their dress is the result of four hundred years of experiment and experience, and we therefore quote the following from a late work on the subject, recently published in London:—

"Few ladies know how to dress for horse exercise, although there has been a great improvement, so far as taste has been concerned, of late years. As to the head-dress, it may be whatever is in fashion, provided it fits the head so as not to require continual adjustment, often needed when the hands would be better employed with the reins and whip. It should shade from the sun, and, if used in hunting, protect the nape of the neck from rain. The recent fashions of wearing the plumes or feathers of the ostrich, the cock, the capercailzie, the pheasant, the peacock, and kingfisher, in the riding-hats of young ladies, in my humble opinion, are highly to be commended. As to the riding habit, it may be of any color or material, suitable to the wearer and season of the year, but the sleeves must fit rather closely; nothing can be more out of place, inconvenient, and ridiculous, than the wide hanging sleeves which look so well in a drawing-room. For country use, the skirt of the habit may be short, and bordered at the bottom a foot deep with leather. The fashion of a waistcoat of light material for summer, revived from the fashion of last century, is a decided improvement; and so is the over-jacket of cloth or seal-skin for rough weather. It is the duty of every woman to dress in as becoming and attractive a manner as possible; there is no reason why pretty young girls should not indulge in picturesque riding-costume, so long as it is appropriate. Many ladies entirely spoil the 'set' of their dress skirts, by retaining the usual *impedimenta* of petticoats. The best horsewomen wear nothing more than a flannel chemise, with long, colored sleeves. Ladies trowsers should be of the same material and color as the habit; and, if full, flowing like a Turk's, and fastened with an elastic band round the ankle, they will not be distinguished from the skirt. In this costume, which may be made amply warm by the folds of the trowsers, plaited like a Highlander's kilt (fastened with an elastic band at the waist), a lady can sit down in a manner impossible for one encumbered by two or three short petticoats. It is the chest and back that require double folds of protection during and after stormy exercise. There is a prejudice against ladies wearing long Wellington boots, but it is quite absurd, for they need never be seen, and are a great comfort and protection in riding long distances, when worn with trowsers tucked inside. They should, for obvious reasons, be large enough for warm woolen stockings, and easy to get on and off. It would not look well to see a lady struggling out of a pair of wet boots, with the help of a bootjack and a couple of chambermaids. The heels of riding-boots, whether for ladies or gentlemen, should be low, but long to keep the stirrup in its place."

THE LAWS OF HOME ETIQUETTE.

A Chapter for Every One to Read and to Commit to Memory — How Homes are made Models of Happiness and Comfort — The Laws of Intercourse with Guests and with Members of the Family,

HOW TO ORDER A HOME. — RULES FOR HOME CONDUCT AND FAMILY ETIQUETTE.

As we have said, all *true* politeness is founded in kindness and unselfishness. Nowhere is there a better chance for its better display than in the family circle. Here we may be certain that it springs from genuine goodness, as there is nothing to be gained by its practice, except the reward which comes from all well-doing. We may say that in no place is there so much *need* of its exercise, in order to keep the wheels of life running smoothly; for "family jars," as they are laughingly called, are very apt to occur, unless the oil of kindness is used to subdue the friction. Children should always show their parents that respect and tenderness which is *their due*. Even where they may consider that they have been unjustly dealt with, it is well for them to remember their own inexperience, that, possibly, their judgment may not be as perfect as they now believe it to be; and that, at all events, the love and care bestowed upon them, in the helpless days of their childhood, entitle their parents to regard and consideration.

For children to place their parents in a ridiculous light before others, mocking their defects, or appearing too conscious of their old-fashioned manners, is only a proof of their own weakness, and will lessen them in the esteem of any amiable person.

For children to assume the most comfortable chairs, the most conspicuous places, or, in any way, to intrude themselves first, to the neglect of then parents, is a very grave fault.

It is desirable to take the first step in the courtesies of the day, which engender so much pleasant feeling, by meeting the different members of the family with a cheerful "Good-morning."

It is highly desirable that, at table, the same rules of precedence, the same moderation and nicety be observed which would be practiced if guests were present. Fixed *habits* of politeness will only be attained where they are cultivated *at home*.

No scrambling, haste, untidiness, or noise should be allowed among the younger members of the circle. They should be made to wait quietly until their elders are served, to eat without unseemly greediness, and drink without labored breathing or spasmodic sounds. If early trained to propriety, it will not be necessary to banish them from the table every time that company is present. Such banishment will tend to make them awkward and lacking in self-possession; though, of course, well-governed children will wait cheerfully when there is necessity for it.

A pleasant "thank you," or "I'm obliged to you," spoken by one sister to another, to a brother, or a mother, for a favor conferred, will last, even in a selfish point of view; for it will increase the *disposition to be kind*, and will lighten the burden of any little service unmistakably. Children should never press around a visitor with the question, "How long are you going to stay?" nor around a relative or parent, returned from an absence, with, "What have you brought me?" "Did you bring me any thing pretty?" If they have reason to expect a present, let them refrain from alluding to it, lest the friend should suspect they thought more of the gift than of welcoming the giver.

If a new member enters the family, as the bride of a brother, or the husband of a sister, true good-breeding can never appear to better advantage, than in the kind reception and treatment of the new-comer. Ideas and habits in such an one, differing from those of the circle into which he or she may have come, should not be too severely criticised; for, it should be remembered, they have probably been differently educated. Even faults should be as charitably viewed as possible; and where respect and love are impossible, it is still best for those who *must* dwell together, to exercise Christian forbearance, and not forget such courtesies as the case admits of.

If you have invited guests, forget your own pleasure in consulting theirs; never do or say a rude thing to a guest. Many a jest, sarcasm, inattention, or slight, which would be excusable anywhere else, becomes a rudeness if it happens under your own roof to a person calling upon or visiting you. Even in a friendly argument, be careful not to forget yourself, and take sides too warmly *against* your opponent, if he be also your visitor or guest.

If you have extended a special invitation to a friend at a distance to come and remain with you for a time, if the friend be a lady, and arrives by any public conveyance, have yourself, your carriage, or some messenger at the spot of arrival to conduct her to your residence. The house should be in good order, that she may not feel disconcerted, nor that she is an intruder. Have all things prepared to give her a cheerful welcome. Let her not suffer from the neglect to provide for her comfort those things which she would not like to be compelled to ask for. Her room should be well supplied with the means of bathing and refreshing herself, and for arranging her toilet. The bureau should have empty drawers for the accommodation of her muslins, and the closet empty pegs for the reception of her dresses. She should be consulted as to the *kind* of bed she prefers, and allowed to retire early, the first evening, if fatigued with her journey. As some people are in the habit of sleeping under more covering than others, there should be a certainty of plenty, especially if the weather be chilly or changeable.

She should be made to feel *welcome*, and be honored by such civilities as will please her. If she is fond of company, and expects to be introduced to your circle of friends, you should apprise your friends in advance of her visit, that they may call upon her after her arrival.

The table should be neat and furnished with suitable dishes. Of course, your means and habits, will influence the amount of expense and trouble you can afford to go to; what we mean is, that a guest should not be left to feel neglected or un-cared for. We have said "lady," in speaking of the visitor; but the same rules will be observed toward guests of the other sex; only they are not usually so much in the house, do not absorb so much of your time, nor require so much company. The gentleman of the house will see that his friend is amused and cared for when out with him during those hours not usually spent at home.

Do not allow your children to be troublesome to visitors; to climb upon them, soil their dresses with their fingers, handle their jewelry and ornaments, ask an-noying questions, nor intrude themselves into their private apartments at unsea-sonable hours; nor ever, without first knocking and waiting to be bidden to come in. Do not, yourself, intrude without knocking; nor allow your servants to do so.

To permit children to ask visitors for money, or for articles in their possession, which the children may admire, is extremely out of place.

To permit children to follow company about, never giving them a moment of retirement, standing by while they make their toilet, and at all times and seasons, is not only annoying, but is vulgar.

If you have invited a friend or friends to tea, have every thing in readiness by the earliest hour at which they may be expected. Do not let them find fires just lighted, yourself not dressed, nor other evidences that they have arrived too soon.

Usually guests—especially ladies—will desire to lay aside their outer gar-ments in some dressing-room, where they can give a glance at their hair, or ar-range their dress, before being ushered into the parlor. If you have asked a gentle-man friend, whom you knew has just come from his place of business, give him an opportunity of bathing his face and hands, and brushing his hair.

There are many little attentions to the entertainment and comfort of others which will not be wanting where the will is good and the heart sincere. *Try to make all feel at ease and happy in your house.*

While every attention is counseled to be shown to guests, let it not be supposed that *show* and *seeming*, to "keep up appearances" before others, is what is sought.

The inmates of the same house should endeavor to be agreeable to one an-other. No outside admiration can compensate for the want of love and respect at home. Gross neglect of attire, unseemly morning apparel, uncombed hair, and total neglect of those little arts and charms which make the female portion of the household so much more lovable, are inexcusable. We should bear in mind that the love of friends is worth more than the flattery of strangers. Only absolute ill-health, or great stress of employment, can excuse slovenly appearances at *any* hour of the day, in any member of the family.

The table should *always* be laid with a certain degree of care. Dishes should not be huddled on, nor dirty table-linen allowed, because there is no company to criticise. This will be one of the *surest tests* of the refinement of a family.

The birthdays of the different members should be honored with good wishes; and gifts, however trifling, if affectionately given, help to keep up that kindly feeling which is the life of the social circle.

It is well to have a few feast-days in the course of the year. Life was not made entirely for labor; and an occasional holiday is a bright spot for children to look back to when they are no longer children. This is only *a hint*—we would not assert it to be "etiquette."

While children should honor their parents, parents should never seek to humiliate or degrade their children. It is bad policy to assert to a child, "You were always bad," "There is no good in you," "You are a liar," or, "You have disgraced yourself beyond forgiveness." Teach your children to respect *your* moderation, if you wish them to govern *their* passions. Teach them to respect themselves, if you wish them to possess any manliness or sense of honor.

Never *scold*. Administer reproof in a calm manner; it will be much more effective, while it will not fail to preserve the respect of your servants and children much more successfully and satisfactorily than the harsher course.

If visitors call when it is impossible or very inconvenient for you to see them, do not be afraid to send word that you are engaged. They have no right to be offended. Better far to tell the truth than to send the false and silly message, that you are "not at home."

CARDS OF INVITATION, WEDDING CARDS, ETC.

The Formulas of Invitations, Cards of Address, Calling Cards, Wedding Cards, Letters of Introduction, etc., etc.

In inviting persons to an evening party, the form is: "Mrs. E. would be pleased to see Mr. and Mrs. D. at her house, on Thursday evening;" or, "Mrs. E.'s compliments to Mr. and Mrs. D., for Thursday evening;" or, "Mrs. E. at home on Thursday evening;" addressing the envelope to Mr. and Mrs. D.

If to a dinner-party, the form is much the same, only the hour is added, thus: "Mrs. E. at home Thursday evening. Dinner at six o'clock." In case the hour is named, the guest commits a great discourtesy in not being on hand at that hour precisely.

If a dance is proposed, it is proper to word the invitation, so as to inform the invited of the fact, thus: "Mrs. E.'s compliments for Thursday evening, to music and dancing;" or, "Mrs. E. will be pleased to see her friends, Thursday, at 8 P. M., to a dance."

When it is a public ball, or a stated soiree, the form of invitation is more formal: "Your company is solicited to a ball (or soiree, or party dansante), to be given at the Metropolitan Rooms, on the evening of Thursday, Dec. 10th, 1860." Then follow the names of the managing committee. This invitation should always be sent at least one week beforehand, in order to give ladies time to prepare their dresses.

If it is impossible from sickness, or otherwise, to accept an invitation to a private party, an excuse, or declination, should invariably be sent in on the *day prior* to the party, that the lady of the house may be advised as to who is coming and who is not. This is a rule too little observed, but a really necessary one, to be made the study of all to practice. For a gentleman not to attend a party, after having received an invitation, and to send in no excuse for absence, is to be construed into a designed "cut," or as an evidence of ignorance. In many cases—particularly in cities—the rule is to send in notes of acceptance of invitation; but this is a superfluous ceremony, when it is understood that silence gives consent. The form of a declination of invitation is: "Mr. and Mrs. D. regret their inability to attend upon Mrs. E.'s invitation for Thursday evening." Or, when a good excuse is desirable, say: "Mr. and Mrs. D. greatly regret that sickness (or other and prior engagements) will prevent their acceptance of Mrs. E.'s kind invitation for Thursday evening."

In all cases of invitations or declinations, the date of writing should be placed on the left hand, below.

A plain, satin surfaced note paper, should be used, and the note should be inclosed in an envelope prepared for note paper, and be directed simply: "Mr. and Mrs. D.—Present;" and if sons and daughters are invited out of the same household, separate invitations should be sent to each. If a person is worth inviting at all, it is but proper that a *whole note* should be inclosed. In case of husband and wife, as the law pronounces them "one," a single note will serve for both.

For visiting cards, the custom changes often. Sometimes it is a glazed card, sometimes not; sometimes a large one, sometimes a small one; sometimes with silvered edges, sometimes with golden border; sometimes with printed inscription, sometimes engraved, sometimes written in pencil. Any person designing to get up a set of visiting or wedding cards, should consult a good engraver; or, if no such person is near, should obtain from some friend, "just from the Metropolis," the "style." The usual form for visiting cards, is simply the name, no address being given, as that belongs to business. For wedding cards, the style now in vogue is two cards in one envelop, one inscribed with the lady's maiden name, the other with the name of husband and wife, thus: "Mr. and Mrs. John Dean." If these are sent out before the wedding, and are designed as invitations to the ceremony, there is added to the last-named card the words: "At home, Thursday morning, at ten o'clock;" or, as the case may be, in the evening; or, if at church, say: "At St. John's Church, at 10 A. M., Thursday."

Letters of introduction have before been referred to. They should say: "The bearer, Mr. Horatio Green, is solicitous of your acquaintance (or friendship, or advice, or good offices, as the case may be), and I take pleasure in commending him to your favorable attention." In the envelope, along with the introductory note, should be the card of the person introduced.

Neither letters of introduction, nor cards of invitation, should be sealed, except they must be transmitted by mail, in which case reinclose the whole in another envelope for the mail.

Lector House believes that a society develops through a two-fold approach of continuous learning and adaptation, which is derived from the study of classic literary works spread across the historic timeline of literature records. Therefore, we aim at reviving, repairing and redeveloping all those inaccessible or damaged but historically as well as culturally important literature across subjects so that the future generations may have an opportunity to study and learn from past works to embark upon a journey of creating a better future.

This book is a result of an effort made by Lector House towards making a contribution to the preservation and repair of original ancient works which might hold historical significance to the approach of continuous learning across subjects.

HAPPY READING & LEARNING!

LECTOR HOUSE LLP
E-MAIL: lectorpublishing@gmail.com